God Desires

Worship

From His People

God Desires

Worship

From His People

Volume 2

By
Farley Dunn

THIS IS A MYCHURCHNOTES.NET BOOK
TOGETHER WITH THREE SKILLET PUBLISHING
(www.ThreeSkilletPublishing.com)

COPYRIGHT © 2017 BY FARLEY DUNN

www.mychurchnotes.net

God Desires Worship From His People/Farley Dunn – 1st ed.

Vol. 2

This is an original work created by
Farley Dunn for the website MyChurchNotes.net.

All rights reserved.

ISBN: 978-1-943189-42-7

Non-public domain scripture quotations are from The Holy Bible, English Standard Version® (ESV®), copyright © 2001 by Crossway, a publishing ministry of Good News Publishers. Used by permission. All rights reserved.

Dedication

For my good friends at Apple Mountain Resort in Georgia. This book came about during my week with you.

MyChurchNotes.net

Table of Contents

A Thanksgiving Feast	19
Blessing the Lord	27
Burst Forth into Praise	33
Butter for Our Lord	39
Electrified in Christ	45
Five Opportunities to Praise Christ	51
Getting to the Bare Wood	59
Jealous for Our Love	65
Living Life as a Boaz	71
Love Letters to Our Lord	77
Our Bloodied Knees	83
Our Double Portion	89
Out of Our Cocoon	95
Our Praise Basket	101
Our Tambourine Celebration	107
Our Vision of God	113
Radical Rejoicing	119
Reading God in the Stars	125
The Abundance of Christ	131
The Cheering Section	137
The Smoke of Our Devotion	143

Three-Part Harmony	149
What Do We Owe God?	155
Whom Do We Worship?	161
Coming to Christ in Three Easy Steps	165

Introduction

Worship is designed to move our hearts.

There are days we need that. The discomforts of life weigh us down, and we can't seem to find our way out of the muck. We carry it with us at work, in our cars, and at home.

Even in the church.

A good worship leader lifts us out of that and lets us focus on God. Worship is more than just singing a hymn or two. It's releasing the burdens of our work-a-day world and stepping into the praise house of our Father.

We don't need that just on Sunday morning, either. We need that uplifting every day of the week. How can we get that? By living a life focused on God.

That's more difficult than it sounds.

This set of 24 essays on finding your worshipful spirit in Christ is a good jumpstart. Read them. Enjoy them. Put the lessons they espouse into practice. You'll see a difference in your life, and God will see a difference in your love for him.

Farley Dunn

Light Bulb Moment

When we come to God with a thankful heart, we will leave stuffed, for the victory he promises us will be ours.

A Thanksgiving Feast

THANKSGIVING as we know it is a distinctly American holiday. Although a handful of other countries have Thanksgiving holidays, none are celebrated in the same manner or for the same reasons as in America.

Our Thanksgiving is a grand feast, accompanied by the camaraderie of friends and family—and a little football on the side. Schools shut down, people often travel halfway across the country, and we all finish the day stuffed to the gills.

All in the name of Thanksgiving.

Colossians 1:3-8 is our Thanksgiving meal. The turkey is there, together with the mouthwatering side dishes, down to the dessert that we can barely resist.

Even our game of football is available for us to enjoy.

Let's see how this passage stacks up next to our treasured American holiday.

First, we come with a thankful heart.

> Thanksgiving is exactly what it says. We come to give thanks for all that we have received in life. We have breath in our lungs, food for our tongues, and companionship for our lonely hours.
>
> Paul gives thanks for exactly the same things, for it is with the breath of God that life is breathed into us; he is our eternal source of sustenance; and it is in the cross that we find our companionship in him.
>
> Paul writes with appreciation for all that God has done for this body of believers, and he wants them to know his feelings. He desires them to know they are loved.

Second, we partake of food prepared by another's loving hand.

> The Thanksgiving meal gives its greatest pleasure to the one whose hand has not prepared the

table. Rather, it is in the savory aromas and the beautifully set table that we find our joy in the meal. If our hands do the preparation, sometimes all we can see is the work involved, and we miss the beauty that the meal has become.

Paul did not found the church at Colosse. Rather, it was founded by Epaphras. That gave Paul a unique perspective toward the Colossians. He was able to see the beauty of the meal, rather than the backbreaking work that had gone into its preparation. He states, "I have heard of your faith . . . and the love which you have for all the saints."

Paul takes special pleasure in this body of believers, because he sees them as they really are: a savory aroma rising before God Almighty.

Third, we anticipate the dessert that is to come.

At a Thanksgiving feast, desserts abound. They draw our attention as moths to a flame, even as the turkey arrives on its gleaming platter. Although we are not yet allowed to indulge these most tempting treats, nothing can expunge them from our thoughts.

Paul glories in the feast that is the church at Colosse. Yet, he also anticipates dessert. He knows there is a hope laid up for them in heaven. They have expressed faith in Christ, shown love to those who are like believers, and now can grasp the hope that is to come.

Paul even tells them where the dessert table is located. It is to be found "in the Word of the Truth of the Gospel."

Fourth, we enjoy the company of family and friends.

Without the company of our family and friends, Thanksgiving is nothing more than another plate of food to fill our stomachs for a time. Thanksgiving is what it is because of memories renewed, bonds that are strengthened, and love that grows in our hearts.

Paul recognized that in his letter to the Colossians. The message of the Christ that had come to them through Epaphras now connected this group of believers to the rest of the world, for they shared in the truth of the Christ, and their faith would continue to bring forth fruit, as it had already done.

Paul knew what many had yet to learn. God's

grace only operates in the presence of truth. The church at Colosse had learned this lesson early, and it now strengthened them, fostering love in their hearts.

Fifth, we gather for the game, expecting our favored team to be victorious.

> Football is a vicarious affair. There are few people who can sit to a Thanksgiving meal, and on the same day, rise to battle on the gridiron. Rather, we prefer to loosen our belts and let the pros have at it. In addition, it saves our muscles, keeping the bruises and abrasions of the game underneath someone else's jersey.
>
> Paul praises a faithful companion of the Gospel, one the believers at Colosse held in high esteem. He marches Epaphras onto the field in his pads and helmet, a victor in the Game of Salvation. He is the Colossians' hero, their champion on the field, for he is the one who brought the message of the Christ to Colosse.
>
> Our Christianity is not vicarious, but to associate with one who has achieved success in the Lord builds us up, also.

Sixth, we cheer for the victor, claiming his triumph

as our own.

> The television is on, and the game comes to a head. In the final moments of the final quarter, men leap to their feet, cheering the victor on the screen. There is no embarrassment, nor is there any hesitation in making our enthusiasm known. We want everyone to be aware that we chose the winning side.
>
> Paul knew he was on the winning side, and he championed those who fought his same fight. He raises Epaphras high, for as he champions Epaphras before the body at Colosse, so has Epaphras championed the body before Paul.
>
> It is the love produced by the Spirit of God that makes the victory possible. Paul recognizes that, and when we have our eyes opened, we will also know that there is only one way to become the victor. It is to fight with the Love of Christ as our banner and our sword.

When we come to God with a thankful heart, we will leave stuffed, for the victory he promises us will be ours.

When we become mature Christians,
we want God to feel loved, too.

Blessing the Lord

WATCH a three-year-old. At that tender age, everything is about them. They have no true concept of others except as a fragment of their own world. Mommy goes out the door, and Mommy is gone. Mommy walks back in, and Mommy is there again.

At three, a child is just beginning to see past who they are, but it's not real for them yet. We want our three-year-old to love us, and it's endearing when they say so, but it often comes only when we prompt them. It's how kids are. They have to mature before they can truly understand us as individuals and express mature emotions that are meaningful in a deep way. Their world is all about them, and everything else is part of the glittering kaleidoscope that makes up their days.

It's the same with a new Christian. It's all about them. They feel good when they come to Christ, and that makes their new walk of faith wonderful. However, when God steps away for a time, God is gone forever, it seems. Then when God walks back in, all is wonderful again. Even their praises are interconnected with what God does for them. It's the way new Christians are. They have to mature before they can truly understand God as a true heavenly father and express love to him in a meaningful way.

The first part of 2 Chronicles 20:26 says that the children of Israel gathered in the Valley of Beracah, and there they blessed the Lord.

Read that again. They didn't ask the Lord for anything. Rather, they offered something to God.

How often are our prayers filled with hurt, pain, and demands for God to do something for us? Then when he doesn't come through, he becomes our punching bag?

Maybe we're still immature Christians. Maybe we're still three, and God is waiting patiently for us to mature into adult Christians who can understand God as our heavenly father, and not as one fragment of the kaleidoscope of events that makes up our days.

Paul's words in Romans 11:36 show his maturity in his walk with the Lord:

> "For from him and through him and to him are all things. To him be glory forever. Amen."

When we grow up in Christ, our prayers will become more than repeated requests for gifts from God. We will want to bless him with our words, our love, and our lives, simply because he's there.

When we become mature Christians, we want God to feel loved, too.

Light Bulb Moment

Once we get our eyes off the distractions, we'll discover the hand of Jesus reaching out to us.

Burst Forth into Praise

WHAT makes us sing?

Try this on for size. Posted on August 15, 2015, on sunnyskyz.com, a video clip shows a young Southern Right Whale swimming up to a small fishing boat in Sydney's Middle Harbor. The whale rises out of the water to allow a teenage boy to remove a wad of plastic attached to a fishing line from the corner of its mouth. Once it's gone, the whale repeatedly slaps its fin on the water in appreciation.

Does that do the trick? A young whale and a young human, different species, working together for the same goal?

The Bible tells us in Psalm 28:7:

> "The Lord is my strength and my shield; in him my heart trusts, and I am helped; my heart

exults, and with my song I give thanks to him."

We are like that whale. We have sin stuck to us, and we can't remove it. Our only answer is to rise out of what surrounds us, and find someone who has an ability we don't.

We have to look to Christ.

What was that whale thinking when it came to that boat? Did it see the underside of the craft and think, Ah, the big flat thing with the churning propeller thing is just what I need to solve my problem?

Undoubtedly not.

Rather, that whale looked past the bottom of the boat, and it saw the outstretched hand of the teenager reaching out. It saw its help in the boy's hand and not in the boy's boat.

How often do we see the flaws in the religions of the world, and we allow the flaws to distract us from the Christ? If that whale had focused on the propeller, it would still be carrying that wad of plastic and fishing line in its mouth. Instead, it went for the hand, and then it burst forth into praise, repeatedly slapping its fin as it sang for joy.

Our salvation is all about Christ, not the Church or the world's religions. Once we find him, we'll shout for the joy we find in our salvation.

Once we get our eyes off the distractions, we'll discover the hand of Jesus reaching out to us.

Light Bulb Moment

When we don't expect it back is when we know we've truly given something to God.

Butter for Our Lord

MAKING butter takes work. Churning it by hand is an exacting process, laborious in its intensity, and tiring in the extreme.

Once we start, we have to finish the process, or our butter-making process will fail.

Why is it so hard? We literally have to break apart the milk fat to release the fatty substance that makes up the butter. We drain off the resulting buttermilk, and we are left with creamy butter.

It takes work to create something wonderful for the Lord. We can't just milk the cow. We have to process the milk before we present it to our God.

Genesis 18:8 tells of Abraham's meeting with the angels of the Lord:

> "Then he took curds and milk and the calf that

he had prepared, and set it before them. And he stood by them under the tree while they ate."

Abraham prepared the meal, but he didn't participate in its consumption. He waited to the side, giving butter to the Lord. His butter was the result of the labors of his hands, offered unto God, not in self-indulgence, but in self-sacrifice.

God has given us our example by doing the same for us.

Genesis 1:29 tells of his gift of sustenance:

> "And God said, 'Behold, I have given you every plant yielding seed that is on the face of all the earth, and every tree with seed in its fruit. You shall have them for food.'"

God created the plants, the seeds, and the fruit. He churned the butter, and he stood by as we consumed. When that wasn't enough, he went further.

Isaiah 9:6 tells us:

> "For to us a child is born, to us a son is given; and the government shall be upon his shoulder, and his name shall be called Wonderful Counselor, Mighty God, Everlasting Father, Prince of Peace."

The ultimate butter was served. The smoothest confection. The cream of the crop. Jesus was come to minister unto the world.

What's the butter we offer to the Lord? What do we take that is ours, shake it up to bring out its best, and lay it at the Lord's feet to let him partake while we stand under a nearby tree?

What do we offer to God that we don't expect him to give back? That's what makes up butter for our Lord.

When we don't expect it back is when we know we've truly given something to God.

Light Bulb Moment

When we return God's love to him through our prayers of thanksgiving is when his power truly begins to flow through us.

Electrified in Christ

ARE WE an AC Christian or a DC Christian?

These are electrical terms, describing alternating current and direct current. They have very different properties. As followers of Christ, we are either one or the other.

AC power changes direction periodically. That means that electricity flows one direction across the line, then reverses and flows the other direction. Increasing the voltage of AC transmissions allows the power to be transmitted over very long distances with little power loss.

It's also less complicated to produce AC power. The generators are simpler and easier to maintain. The higher voltages of AC power are necessary to run rare gas lighting, such as today's CFL lights. Then we come to wireless technology. It would be impossible without alternating current.

DC power is different in almost every way. It flows only one direction—from the source to the consumer—fades quickly over long distances, and requires high-maintenance generators. DC doesn't carry the voltage to run modern lighting or wireless devices.

If we want God to always supply us with the bounty of his kingdom, and we aren't giving back to him, we are DC Christians. Once we walk out of the church doors, the power of Christ in us will begin to fade. We won't light up the world, and we can't talk to God wirelessly, because our DC power supply won't support prayer outside of the church building.

As an AC Christian, we give back to God. We sense his presence all around us every moment of the day, and our prayers? We know they work, and we send them heaven's way daily. It doesn't matter if we're in the church or outside. Christ is just as real to us on the job, when we're on vacation, or out mowing the lawn as he is sitting under the ministry of our pastor.

Isaiah 43:24 warns against the DC Christian:

"You have not bought me sweet cane with money, or satisfied me with the fat of your sacrifices. But you have burdened me with your sins; you have wearied me with your iniquities."

Exodus 30:29 tells of the power that will flow from the AC Christian:

"You shall consecrate [all that your hands touch], that they may be most holy. Whatever touches them will become holy."

AC or DC? How we live will tell the sort of Christian we are.

When we return God's love to him through our prayers of thanksgiving is when his power truly begins to flow through us.

Light Bulb Moment

There is no time in our lives that God is not walking beside us. He deserves our praise each and every moment of each and every day.

Five Opportunities to Praise God

TOO MANY times we are like the rat on the wheel. We are so busy asking from God that we hardly have time to offer him praise for the good gifts he gives us.

In the Old Testament, we find where God shows us five opportunities where we should set aside our wheel in order to take the time to offer our praises to him.

Opportunity #1:

> Jacob loved Rachel, but due to her father's trickery, Jacob was forced to marry Rachel's older sister, Leah, before he was able to marry the woman he loved.

Leah knew she wasn't Jacob's first choice. Worse, she felt hated. In Genesis 29:35 we read that God opened her womb, and she bore four sons. The fourth one she named Judah, which means "praise."

When God answers our most fervent prayers, we should offer our praises up to him.

Opportunity #2:

In Leviticus 19:23-25 God laid out a business plan for the Israelites. All profits from the fruit trees they planted were to be untouched for the first three years and sowed into God's kingdom with praise and thanksgiving on the fourth. Only during the fifth year were they allowed to eat of the fruit.

That is a business model we can still count on today. For the first three years, invest all profits back into the company. In the fourth, offer God the firstfruits in thanksgiving, for it is by his hand that our business becomes profitable. In the fifth year, we can reap God's rewards by enjoying the fruits of our labor.

When God has his hand on our business ventures, he deserves praise from us.

Opportunity #3:

Canaan had come mightily against Israel, for without proper spiritual leadership, the children of Israel had become evil in God's sight. The prophetess Deborah announced God's commands to the people, and they listened, offering themselves to be used of God.

We read in Judges 5:2 of the first lines of Deborah's song of triumph against the defeated king of Canaan.

"Praise you the Lord for the avenging of Israel . . ."

When we allow ourselves to be used of God, and he gives us victory over our oppressors, we should sing a song of praise unto him.

Opportunity #4:

The Ark of the Covenant was the most revered relic in Jewish possession. It symbolized the might and glory of Israel.

David had a special place built for the Ark. He offered burnt offerings and sacrifices, and then he gave to each man and woman in Israel food to eat and wine to drink.

1 Chronicles 16:4 says that during this celebration, David appointed men to praise the Lord God of Israel.

When we gather together with our Christian brothers in fellowship and rejoicing, we should take time to lift our praises before the Lord.

Opportunity #5:

The children of Israel had traveled from Canaan to Egypt, where they grew from a group of 30 to about 4 million, and while fleeing back to their homeland, they weathered many mighty and fearsome wonders underneath the guiding hand of God.

Deuteronomy 10:21 tells the children of Israel to look back on what their eyes have seen, and lift their praises to the God of all creation.

When we grow old and look back upon our lives, we should lift our hands in a shout of praise, for we will see the touch of God on every phase of our journey.

There is no time in our lives that God is not walking beside us. He deserves our praise each and every moment of each and every day.

Light Bulb Moment

Let's raise our hands and let the glory of Christ shine to all the world.

Getting to the Bare Wood

ARTISANS love old wood. Antique windows can be repurposed into coffee tables, old doors into room dividers, and collapsing barns into decorative wall finishes.

We can leave the original varnish if we want our repurposed wood to look old, and that adds character to our finished project. With floors, however, it's another thing altogether. We want to get to the bare wood, an undamaged surface, before we set our furniture and rugs on our repurposed floorboards. Otherwise, we'll snag our socks and track paint chips throughout the house.

God needs to get us back to bare wood, also. He needs to strip away the worn finishes of our sinful past, going through a dozen paint layers if necessary. He sands them away to create beauty in us. If, like repurposed wood, we still show marks of our past, they are the exquisite reminders of the hand of the Lord polishing us to perfection. It's the shine of our salvation shimmering across the scars of the world that reflect the majesty of God's resurrection power.

Hebrews 1:1-4 reveals the pumice stone God uses to bring out the beauty of his purpose in our lives:

> "Long ago, at many times and in many ways, God spoke to our fathers by the prophets, but in these last days he has spoken to us by his Son, whom he appointed the heir of all things, through whom also he created the world.
>
> "He is the radiance of the glory of God and the exact imprint of his nature, and he upholds the universe by the word of his power.
>
> "After making purification for sins, he sat down at the right hand of the Majesty on high, having become as much superior to angels as the name he has inherited is more excellent than theirs."

How will the world know we are repurposed in Christ? We find that in Hebrews 1:6:

> "When he brings the firstborn into the world, he

says, 'Let all God's angels worship him.' "

Our heartfelt worship of the Savior will be proof of our new lives in him. After all, if the very angels of the heavens are to worship our almighty God, how can mankind do any less? If we're Christians professing a new life in Jesus, we have no other choice.

Let's raise our hands and let the glory of Christ shine to all the world.

Light Bulb Moment

God needs our love to be voluntary and from the heart. He will respond in kind to our outpouring of love toward him.

Jealous for Our Love

WE CAN choose to believe in whatever God we want. Name it, claim it, yeah, that's one version. Court judge, ready to drop the gavel. That's another. Hands off observer, unwilling to interfere...many people see God in this fashion.

God allows us this choice. He permits us to follow after any version of him we want. He doesn't want little robots walking the earth, all raising their arms at the same time to repeat, "God is good . . .," just because he flips some imaginary toggle switch. He wants us to learn his true nature and worship him because we are emotionally connected to him.

There's a story about a man who reluctantly agrees to turn off the TV, help his wife clear away the dinner dishes, and clean the kitchen. She bursts into tears and tells him to go back and watch TV. Confused, he asks what's wrong. She reveals that it's not help with the dishes that she needs. She needs him to *want* to help with the dishes.

That's God and us. It's not about following all the rules in the Bible. That's important, and we can't discount it, but there's more. If we follow all the proscribed do's and don'ts, and we drag our feet the entire time, God's not interested. He desires us to *want* to follow his rules.

Exodus 20:1-26 reveals how much God needs our interest in him to come from our heart:

> "And God spoke all these words, saying, 'I am the Lord your God, who brought you out of the land of Egypt, out of the house of slavery. You shall have no other gods before me. You shall not make for yourself a carved image, or any likeness of anything that is in heaven above, or that is in the earth beneath, or that is in the water under the earth. You shall not bow down to them or serve them, for I the Lord your God am a jealous God, visiting the iniquity of the fathers on the children to the third and the fourth gen-

eration of those who hate me . . .' "

We find out more about God in this passage, revealing each of the Ten Commandments, but the essence of his nature is clear in these beginning verses. God is jealous for our love. He wants us to view him in the same way he sees us, as objects of his adoration, people for whom he is willing to do all manner of wondrous things. God wants us to *want* to show our love unto him.

God needs our love to be voluntary and from the heart. He will respond in kind to our outpouring of love toward him.

Light Bulb Moment

We are loved because we're loved, not because of what we do for God.

Living Life as a Boaz

GOD DOESN'T need us.

That's a jaw-shattering thought. We want to feel necessary. We need to be important in other people's plans. If we're useless, then we're no more than peripheral baggage. We're out of the line of sight, and we're easily forgotten.

Yet God loves us beyond all compare.

The two most prominent features of the temple built in Solomon's time were twin pillars of brass set into the temple's porch. 1 Kings 7:21 tells us the right pillar was named Jachin, meaning "he shall establish," and the left pillar was named Boaz, or "strength."

The pillars gave no support to the temple, yet they

rested in a place of significance. On the east side of the temple, they caught the morning sun, and it gleamed on the polished brass.

It must have been glorious to behold.

God sees us the same. His creation will endure whether we are here or we're not. The clouds will continue to fill the sky, the oceans will break upon the shore, and the moon will rise in the sky. We control none of that.

Even so, surrounded by the majestic beauty of his creation, God desired more, and he created man. He set us up as the pinnacle of his creation in the most prominent location possible. He set us up to shine before him.

He named us, and we carry the pedigree of strength through his eternal word.

The problem with brass is that it tarnishes easily. The mirror-like shine is obscured bit by bit until the tarnish becomes all we can see. It's why God has to continually polish us back to brilliance with his loving hand.

He's intentionally set us up in a position that shows us off, and he wants us to shine before the world. He finds his joy in us, and he wants to share that with every facet of his creation.

We are the shining pillars on the porch of his creation, placed at the forefront of God's house, and loved by God above all else he's made.

We are loved because we're loved, not because of what we do for God.

Light Bulb Moment

We trigger God's love to us when we first offer our love to him.

Love Letters to Our Lord

WE ALL have an opinion about love, about what it is, how it makes us feel, and what it means to not experience it.

Helen Keller, famous American spokeswoman, said, "The best and most beautiful things in this world cannot be seen or even heard, but must be felt with the heart."

For those of us who are unfamiliar with Helen Keller, at a very early age she lost both her hearing and her sight. She was an expert on what the important things were. She could only feel, and she did it best with her heart.

Johann Wolfgang von Goethe, German writer and statesman, once famously said, "We are shaped and fashioned by those we love."

Yet we only know we are loved in return when someone tells us so.

When we tell our Father in heaven we love him, we become the most beautiful thing in all creation to him, and that shapes who he is. He wraps his love around us, because we call out our love to him.

Let's exalt our Most High God with Love Letters of Praise!

Psalm 99:5 tells us:

> "Exalt the Lord our God; worship at his footstool! Holy is he!"

1 Chronicles 16:29 says:

> "Ascribe to the Lord the glory due his name; bring an offering and come before him! Worship the Lord in the splendor of holiness."

Judges 5:3 admonishes us:

> "Hear, O kings; give ear, O princes; to the Lord I will sing; I will make melody to the Lord, the God

of Israel."

Psalm 150:1-5 gives us a plan of action:

> "Praise the Lord! Praise God in his sanctuary; praise him in his mighty heavens! Praise him for his mighty deeds; praise him according to his excellent greatness! Praise him with trumpet sound; praise him with lute and harp! Praise him with tambourine and dance; praise him with strings and pipe! Praise him with sounding cymbals; praise him with loud clashing cymbals!"

Mahatma Gandhi, Indian political leader, gave his take on love: "Where there is love there is life."

To turn that around for the Christian, we might say, "When we fall in love with God, he brings us new life."

We trigger God's love to us when we first offer our love to him.

Light Bulb Moment

When we are devoted to Christ, his love will pour over us, and we will know his blessings without end.

Our Bloodied Knees

THE SHRINE of Fatima about 70 miles north of Lisbon Portugal has one of the most distinct provenances of any pilgrimage site in Europe. It does not date from the Middle Ages, but rather from the early 20th century.

Nearly two million people a year visit this site, making it one of the most revered locations in all Europe. On May 13 and October 13, half a million pilgrims crowd the square in front of the basilica. Many have arrived on their bloodied knees. Women often walk on their knees when they near the basilica as a sign of extreme devotion.

Whether we agree with their exhibition of devotion or not (many of the local priests do not) the sincerity of their actions cannot be questioned.

How sincere are we as modern Christians in our devotion to the Christ?

Let's look at four unparalleled Old Testament acts of devotion to God:

Act of Devotion #1:

> Noah built an altar and took one of each of the animals in the ark and offered them to God. Genesis 8:20-22.

Act of Devotion #2:

> Jacob built an altar where God appeared to him, and at the same time, he abandoned all foreign gods. Genesis 35:1-4.

Act of Devotion #3:

> David refused to offer a sacrifice that cost him nothing. 2 Samuel 24:24.

Act of Devotion #4:

> Hezekiah restored the altar that had been desecrated by his father, King Ahaz. 2 Chronicles 29:18-24.

When we are sincere in our devotion to God, and we make a show of our love toward him, it will cost us something. It may be our time, our money, or our standing among our fellow men. However, there will be a price.

Let's look at what we get in return:

God's Outpouring of Love #1:

> God's blessings will flow without end. Genesis 49:26.

God's Outpouring of Love #2:

> There is joy in heaven when we repent. Luke 15:7.

God's Outpouring of Love #3:

> God's Spirit dwells in us. 1 Corinthians 3:16.

God's Outpouring of Love #4:

> We will rise to rule at Jesus' side for a thousand years. Revelation 20:4-6.

The pilgrims who journey to Fatima receive a sense of absolution for their bloodied knees. It's an act of utmost devotion. However, do they receive more than just broken skin and brittle scabs? That's between them and God.

For our acts of devotion, the Bible lists exactly what we can expect. We will be blessed, surrounded with joy, have the Spirit dwell within, and rise at Jesus' side.

That's what we receive for our bloodied knees.

When we are devoted to Christ, his love will pour over us, and we will know his blessings without end.

Light Bulb Moment

Our grateful heart is what draws the mercy of our God unto us in all situations.

Our Double Portion

THE STORY of Pinocchio, written over a hundred years ago, is known worldwide. The boy, not real, and the old man, without a son, are engaging in their appeal for all ages. Geppetto the woodcarver creates a masterpiece, and he wishes on a fallen star for the puppet to come to life.

There are lessons too many to count in this story, so let's pull out just one: Sometimes we can find our blessing in not getting what we want.

Geppetto, the old man, has all the time in the world to do exactly what he wants. He desires a son, even though he knows nothing about parenting. He wants the illusion of something with little concept of exactly what it entails.

Geppetto wants a dream.

When the Blue Fairy gives the woodcarver his wish, an ensuing debacle of disasters takes place, which of course is the point in the story. We laugh along with Pinocchio's misfortunes, and we enjoy the puppet's failures as much or more than when he becomes a real boy.

When God gives us what we want, do we complain that it's not exactly what we thought, or do we enjoy all that comes along with it, understanding that we're getting exactly what we asked for?

In 1 Samuel Chapter 1, Hannah faced Geppetto's challenge. She had no children, and she desperately wanted a child. There was an upside to Hannah's situation. Her husband loved her, even though she had no children, and in 1 Samuel 1:5 we read that her husband gave her a double portion when he went up to sacrifice at Shiloh.

Hannah knew she was loved, even more than her husband's second wife. Yet, she felt distraught at her misfortune.

God granted her desire for a son, but it came with a price. The son was Samuel, and he was to be dedicated to the Lord. He lived in the temple, and he would become a great prophet who led the nation of Israel.

Our double portion sometimes comes in what we do not have. We give up what we possess when we get what we want. Is receiving our heart's desire worth the price we pay, or do we sometimes feel annoyed that God didn't do things exactly right?

Geppetto got the son he desired, but only when he was willing to take the time and interest to parent him properly. Hannah got the son she desired, but he wasn't truly hers. He lived in the temple to be raised by Eli the priest.

When God answers our prayers, do we see the answer, or do we see the challenge that comes along with it? Our double portion comes not in the things we receive, but in how we see the things we receive. God wishes us to be grateful for all things, and to lift our voices in praise unto him.

Our grateful heart is what draws the mercy of our God unto us in all situations.

Light Bulb Moment

When we focus on God, we are always beautiful to him.

Out of Our Cocoon

THE CATERPILLAR doesn't know what's coming. It crawls, eats, and lives a life that seems complete. What more could it want? Then, one day it decides it's had enough, and it burrows away in the security of its retirement cocoon, certain that its life is over and done.

Its cocoon is a prison from which it can never escape. The irony is that the cocoon doesn't entrap the caterpillar. Rather, the caterpillar spins its own private prison bars. One thread at a time, the deed is done, and the creature is bound for all eternity.

Or so it would seem.

God views the walls we build around ourselves differently. We may drive ourselves into debt, and it might be our anger that forces our family to abandon us. Our health issues may very well come from our own raucous and irresponsible lifestyle. These things form our prison walls, trapping us in our misery, and we feel we cannot escape

God doesn't want us to escape.

Don't stop reading here. Think of the caterpillar. It's bound tightly in its cocoon, and to passersby, it seems its life is over. The caterpillar appears dead.

It's not. Inside its prison walls, it's being remade into something more beautiful than it ever could have been had it chosen to retain its freedom as a caterpillar. When its prison walls crumble around it, out crawls the butterfly. It appears broken for a moment, then its glory unfurls, and it becomes the most magnificent of God's creatures.

Think about the children of Israel. They were carried into captivity by the king of Babylon and kept behind bars for seventy years. They must have felt their lives were over, that they would never know the taste of freedom again. But like the caterpillar, they were being remade into something better and more beautiful. Ezra 2:2 begins the list of those who were repatriated to their homeland by Cyrus the king.

Ezra 2:69 tells of the new attitude of the Israelites

when it came time to worship the Lord:

> "They gave after their ability unto the treasury of the work threescore and one thousand drams of gold, and five thousand pounds of silver, and one hundred priests' garments."

The caterpillars had been transformed into butterflies, and as they fluttered their wings in the sunshine of their new freedom, they shimmered in the eyes of God, and he found them magnificent, indeed.

When we focus on God, we are always beautiful to him.

Light Bulb Moment

When we invite Jesus in, praise and glory and peace will also be there.

Our Praise Basket

AT ONE time baskets were the primary method of toting things around. They could be woven from common grasses, and they were very durable. They could be worked tightly and waterproofed, or entwined loosely for good airflow.

Dorothy carried Toto in a basket in *The Wizard of Oz*. Miriam watched over Moses floating in a basket in the book of Genesis. Movie makers love to show snake charmers teasing cobras out of lidded baskets.

What should we load into our spiritual baskets?

James 5:13 tells us:

> "Is anyone among you suffering? Let him pray. Is anyone cheerful? Let him sing praise."

We must store away prayer and praise in our baskets.

Acts 16:25 tells us:

> "About midnight Paul and Silas were praying and singing hymns to God, and the prisoners were listening to them."

Paul and Silas found room for prayer and songs in their baskets.

Luke 2:14 tells us:

> "Glory to God in the highest, and on earth peace among those with whom he is pleased!"

The multitude of the heavenly host filled mankind's baskets with their songs of glory.

Matthew 5:14-16 tells us:

> "You are the light of the world. A city set on a hill cannot be hidden. Nor do people light a lamp and put it under a basket, but on a stand, and it gives light to all in the house. In the same way, let your light shine before others, so that they may see your good works and give glory to your

Father who is in heaven."

When we uncover what's in our basket, it will be seen by all the world.

Zechariah 9:9 tells us:

> "Rejoice greatly, O daughter of Zion! Shout aloud, O daughter of Jerusalem! Behold, your king is coming to you; righteous and having salvation is he, humble and mounted on a donkey, on a colt, the foal of a donkey."

When we have Jesus in our basket, the rest of the world will begin to shout with us, for he is glorious in all his being, the one who is lifted on high.

Psalm 28:7 tells us:

> "The Lord is my strength and my shield; in him my heart trusts, and I am helped; my heart exults, and with my song I give thanks to him."

Blessed is the man who opens his basket and finds the Lord inside.

The design of our basket is unimportant. Loose weave? Tight weave? Maybe even waterproofed...it doesn't matter. What counts is having Jesus inside. That is the important thing.

When we invite Jesus in, praise and glory and peace will also be there.

Light Bulb Moment

When we party for Jesus, that's when the world will understand his majesty and want to join in our victory celebration.

Our Tambourine Celebration

THINK OF a Fourth of July parade, with banners waving, and fireworks lighting up the sky. Imagine a Macy's extravaganza on New Year's Day, weaving through New York City, celebrating a brand-new year.

We love to celebrate. On birthdays, we don paper hats, toot party horns, and generally live it up. Super Bowl parties are a time of feasting, raucous behavior, and general mayhem all around.

We love to attend a good party, because that's where the fun is!

How do we treat God's party? He loves a good celebration, too.

Now that gets a reaction. God as a party animal? Certainly, if we believe the Word of God.

Read the words in Psalm 150:1-5:

> "Praise the Lord! Praise God in his sanctuary; praise him in his mighty heavens! Praise him for his mighty deeds; praise him according to his excellent greatness! Praise him with trumpet sound; praise him with lute and harp! Praise him with tambourine and dance; praise him with strings and pipe! Praise him with sounding cymbals; praise him with loud clashing cymbals!"

Can we wave banners over our heads in celebration of Christ? Certainly! How about fireworks, are they allowed? Bring them on.

A parade, though. That might be a little much, if do say so ourselves. Right? Not on your life! Let's put the Macy's event to shame, making our strut through the streets of the most vibrant city in the world one that people will remember the rest of their lives.

God wants us to don our paper hats, toot our party horns, and generally live it up. Let's look at his words again:

"Praise him with sounding cymbals; praise him with loud clashing cymbals!"

This is a Super Bowl party to end all parties! Let's make this our Tambourine Celebration, with raucous behavior for Jesus, and Christian mayhem all around!

When we finish celebrating how good and how great our Lord is, we want the world to notice, sit up, and say, "Hey, I want some of that! Can I come next time?"

When we party for Jesus, that's when the world will understand his majesty and want to join in our victory celebration.

When we truly see God, we begin to understand how holy he is in every conceivable way.

Our Vision of God

WHO IS our God? How do we envision him? Is he a grandfather, with a halo of white hair, kindly bestowing loving kindness on his progeny?

On the ceiling of the Sistine Chapel, Michelangelo depicts God as a sturdy, muscular man of advancing years, with a gray beard and white hair, telling of his wisdom and great age.

John 4:24 tells us God is of a spirit nature. He has no physical form.

1 John 4:16 says he is love, which includes grace, kindness, and mercy.

1 John 1:5 describes God as a being of light, with no darkness in him.

Exodus 3:2 paints his countenance as a flaming bush in the wilderness.

Genesis 15:17 offers us a vision of God as a flaming torch and a smoking firepot.

Hebrews 12:29 envisions God as a consuming fire, holy and righteous in his nature.

1 Kings 18:38 portrays God as an all-consuming flame, devouring flesh, wood, stones, and dust; and reaching out to lick up the water in the ditch.

When we see God in our minds, do we envision a hefty bank account, a strict school marm, a distant unknowable distraction, or perhaps, in our moments of crisis, a First Responder, there to rescue us from the snares of the world?

God is not as we desire him to be, but as he is. In Isaiah 1:2-3, the Lord despairs over his creation.

> "Children have I reared and brought up, but they have rebelled against me. ...My people do not understand."

Do we understand the true nature of God? Is he our

avenue to financial success and better living; our rescue team when we can't make it on our own; or is he the consuming fire that will one day wipe all sin and degradation from the face of the earth? Perhaps Michelangelo got it right. Our God is the sturdy one, with great strength in his limbs, and in him is the greatest wisdom of all the ages.

Let's envision that God. He's the one the Bible describes, from cover to cover.

When we truly see God, we begin to understand how holy he is in every conceivable way.

Light Bulb Moment

Let's paint our faces with Jesus and get ready to jump and cheer. There's a celebration coming our way!

Radical Rejoicing

IN THE Harry Potter series of movies, Harry has a cousin who is an oaf. His parents dote on him, trying to buy his love with unearned praises and undeserved gifts. At one celebration, the boy counts his gifts, uncaring what they are, only concerned with the quantity of packages.

He screams out his anger: Did he get one more than last time?

Of course, this character is little more than a caricature of the worst a teenage boy can be, but he illustrates today's message especially well. When we are overly blessed, we can grow numb to the good things in life that come our way.

In contrast, Harry, owning nothing and forced to

live under the stairs, gets a simple letter, and he is ecstatic. This one, small item is a gift to him better than gold. When it is taken away, he is devastated.

Harry rejoices when he is finally offered escape from his locked-up lifestyle. His parents are dead. He feels unloved. The possibility of attending boarding school is the open door of freedom to this boy who has known few good things in his short lifetime.

As sinners in this world, we are the same. Jesus said it like this in Luke 7:47:

> "Therefore I tell you, her sins, which are many, are forgiven—for she loved much. But he who is forgiven little, loves little."

It is the person who starts out with nothing that is grateful for every little blessing that comes his or her way. When we hear radical rejoicing going on, we can be assured that we are hearing the sounds of a radically changed life.

Jacob, in Genesis 28:20-22, made a vow, saying:

> "If God will be with me and will keep me in this

way that I go, and will give me bread to eat and clothing to wear, so that I come again to my father's house in peace, then the Lord shall be my God, and this stone, which I have set up for a pillar, shall be God's house. And of all that you give me I will give a full tenth to you."

God proved himself to Jacob, and Jacob lived up to his promises. His family line became a great nation, one that still stands as God's chosen people, even in the face of continual border conflicts and international pressure.

Look at what Revelation 21:4 tells us:

"He will wipe away every tear from their eyes, and death shall be no more, neither shall there be mourning, nor crying, nor pain anymore, for the former things have passed away."

Talk about a good reason for radical rejoicing! No matter what bad things have come our way in this lifetime, it will all be gone. God will wipe every pain away.

We will all stand and cheer when we see the events of that final day come to pass. Will we paint our faces in vibrant colors and wear outrageous clothes as we cheer the coming presence of the great King? Who knows, but it wouldn't be a crazy idea, not when we read the following:

Revelation 19:9 decries:

> "And the angel said to me, 'Write this: Blessed are those who are invited to the marriage supper of the Lamb.' And he said to me, 'These are the true words of God.'"

Revelation 5:13 builds up our expectations:

> "And I heard every creature in heaven and on earth and under the earth and in the sea, and all that is in them, saying, 'To him who sits on the throne and to the Lamb be blessing and honor and glory and might forever and ever!'"

We will hear the true words of God as we sing our praises forever without end!

How radical is that!

Let's paint our faces with Jesus and get ready to jump and cheer. There's a celebration coming our way!

Light Bulb Moment

When the majesty of creation surrounds us, we are enveloped in the loving hands of our fabulous heavenly Father.

Reading God in the Stars

THE HOROSCOPE section of the daily news is consistent in one thing. It never tells us anything specific. It hints, suggests, and offers guidance so vague that we can interpret it just about any way we want.

How would that work in the field of finance? We buy a home, and we sign on the dotted line with only a suggestion of a price hovering out there, one someone will eventually fill in depending on the circumstances of the day.

Or we apply for a new job with no more than a hint of our duties and pay. We wander the building hoping we will eventually find an office, and that we will actually get a real paycheck come Friday.

In actuality, we do this all the time. We spend our

days in the earthly realm, hoping the spiritual one will sort itself out. Ah, reincarnation is the assurance of the moment. Later we think: I was saved as a young girl, so what I do now doesn't matter. Once saved, always saved, after all. Or we don't bother at all, for what God would send his creation to a very real and painful hell? Of course we'll all be in heaven with him.

All we have to do is look up, and we will find the truth in the stars (and that doesn't mean we are to follow the day's horoscope).

Psalm 19:1 tells us "the heavens declare the glory of God, and the sky above proclaims his handiwork."

Matthew 2:2 gives us the wise men's words: "Where is he who has been born king of the Jews? For we saw his star when it rose and have come to worship him."

Jeremiah 10:2 cautions us to "not be dismayed at the signs of the heavens because the nations are dismayed at them."

Genesis 1:16 reminds us that "God made the two

great lights—the greater light to rule the day and the lesser light to rule the night—and the stars."

So, what is this all about? The glory of the Lord, of course. His power is shown in all creation, and when we look at the stars above, we can find finger after finger pointing directly unto him.

We can read of our coming Savior in Luke 21:25-27:

> "And there will be signs in sun and moon and stars, and on the earth distress of nations in perplexity because of the roaring of the sea and the waves, people fainting with fear and with foreboding of what is coming on the world. For the powers of the heavens will be shaken. And then they will see the Son of Man coming in a cloud with power and great glory."

Where is the power in our daily horoscopes? What truth can we find in astrology? The stars are all about Jesus and his Father, the Almighty God of Creation. When we look up, let's look for him. We can read him in the stars.

When the majesty of creation surrounds us, we are enveloped in the loving hands of our fabulous heavenly Father.

Light Bulb Moment

When we lift our hands in praise, the gates of heaven will release the Father's blessing on our lives.

The Abundance of Christ

Take a cup.

Any cup, with or without a handle, one that holds water.

Fill it up. Then add a little more, until the liquid is at the top. Let the surface tension of the water hold it in as the water bulges over the rim yet doesn't overflow.

Finally, one last drop, and the water will spill over, flooding the countertop, and going everywhere.

That's what Christ does in our lives. He fills us up, more and more, and if we remain steady in him, that final drop will cause us to spill Christ all over everything and everyone around us. Christ will go everywhere.

Revelation 1:8 tells us:

> "I am Alpha and Omega, the beginning and the ending, saith the Lord, which is, and which was, and which is to come, the Almighty."

There is no lack in God. He knows no restrictions. He's not limited by our checking account, our education, or our family connections. When he flows into us, he's drawing from the resources of all creation, for it's all his.

Psalm 89:6 reveals his wonder:

> "For who in the heaven can be compared unto the Lord? who among the sons of the mighty can be likened unto the Lord?"

We are weak, but he is filled with wonder and glory. We doubt his favor in our lives, but he desires to love us. We battle with the tumultuous trials of day-to-day living, and all the while, he is with us.

Zephaniah 3:17 reminds us:

> "The Lord your God in the midst of you is mighty; he will save, he will rejoice over you with joy; he will rest in his love, he will joy over

you with singing."

Our great God didn't only create us, he takes joy in his children. He sings over us. He looks down on us, and he throws a party for us, inviting the heavenly host to join in, simply because he can.

We are a cup, waiting to be filled. Christ came so that he could overflow from us onto those around us. Let's get ready for more of him than we can possibly contain.

When we lift our hands in praise, the gates of heaven will release the Father's blessing on our lives.

Light Bulb Moment

God enjoys it when we cheer him on.

The Cheering Section

ON SITCOMS, we cue up the laugh track. At a sports event, we put our hands together. In other situations, we can root someone on, inspire a colleague, or even attend a pep rally.

Say it how we want, if we join in, we are part of the cheering section.

What does a cheering section do? We raise the roof, up the ante, and push those who are hesitant down a new track.

We help them blaze a new trail, to go where no man has gone before.

That last phrase comes from Gene Roddenberry's Star Trek television series from the 1960s.

God's cheering section comes from the time before

time existed.

Revelation 1:8 tells us, " 'I am the Alpha and the Omega,' says the Lord God, 'who is and who was and who is to come, the Almighty.' "

Colossians 1:16 states, "For by him all things were created, in heaven and on earth, visible and invisible, whether thrones or dominions or rulers or authorities—all things were created through him and for him."

John 17:5 relates Jesus' words, "And now, Father, glorify me in your own presence with the glory that I had with you before the world existed."

Psalm 45:6 clarifies God's timeframe beyond a shadow of a doubt: "Your throne, O God, is forever and ever."

With all this, does God even need a cheering section?

Maybe that's the wrong question. Maybe we should ask this instead:

Does God enjoy a cheering section?

And the answer is, apparently, because he has one

in all the angels that inhabit heaven, and in all the saints that have gone before us.

Revelation 19:1 tells of "the loud voice of a great multitude in heaven, crying out, 'Hallelujah! Salvation and glory and power belong to our God!'"

Revelation 19:4 speaks of "the twenty-four elders and the four living creatures [that] fell down and worshiped God who was seated on the throne, saying, 'Amen. Hallelujah!'"

Revelation 19:6 reveals the "voice of a great multitude, like the roar of many waters and like the sound of mighty peals of thunder, crying out, 'Hallelujah! For the Lord our God the Almighty reigns.'"

Revelation 19:7 says, "Let us rejoice and exult and give him the glory, for the marriage of the Lamb has come, and his Bride has made herself ready."

So, what was the party all about? Why were they raising the roof?

We are being invited to the marriage supper of the Lamb. It's the end of time as we know it, the rule of Satan over the earth has come to an end, and we will reside with our God in heaven forever more!

Raise the roof! Yah, yah! Cut in the laugh track, and let's put our hands together! It's time to rouse the cheering section, and give it all we've got!

God enjoys it when we cheer him on.

Light Bulb Moment

It's total commitment that God wants from us. The rest will fall into line as a matter of course.

The Smoke of Our Devotion

In the movie *Mr. Nobody*, the main character Nemo deals with his wife's crushing depression. At one point, she accuses him of taking better care of their car than he does of her.

What does Nemo do? The sensible thing. He pours gasoline over the car and sets it alight. From inside the house, the entire family can see the smoke of his devotion rising into the sky.

How devoted are we to Christ?

Revelation 8:5 reveals the explosive power in following Christ:

> "Then the angel took the censer and filled it with fire from the altar and threw it on the earth, and there were peals of thunder, rumblings, flashes

of lightning, and an earthquake."

Leviticus 16:12 tells of our intimate devotion to him:

"And [Aaron] shall take a censer full of coals of fire from the altar before the Lord, and two handfuls of sweet incense beaten small, and he shall bring it inside the veil."

Hebrews 9:3-4 shows the magnificence our devotion should reflect:

"Behind the second curtain was a second section called the Most Holy Place, having the golden altar of incense and the Ark of the Covenant covered on all sides with gold, in which was a golden urn holding the manna, and Aaron's staff that budded, and the tablets of the covenant."

Ezekiel 8:11 is our call for everyone to participate:

"And before them stood seventy men of the elders of the house of Israel, with Jaazaniah the son of Shaphan standing among them. Each had his censer in his hand, and the smoke of the cloud of incense went up."

1 Kings 7:50 describes the house of our Lord:

> "The cups, snuffers, basins, dishes for incense, and fire pans, of pure gold; and the sockets of gold, for the doors of the innermost part of the house, the Most Holy Place, and for the doors of the nave of the temple."

Numbers 16:39 turns the things of the world into objects of worship for Christ:

> "So Eleazar the priest took the bronze censers, which those who were burned had offered, and they were hammered out as a covering for the altar."

Leviticus 16:13 is God's testament that he brings life, not death, unto all who come to him with a contrite heart.

> "[Aaron shall] put the incense on the fire before the Lord, that the cloud of the incense may cover the mercy seat that is over the testimony, so that he does not die."

When we toss our most prized possessions on the altar of devotion, the smoke of our sacrifice will rise toward heaven, proof of our love for our Father above. What does God want us to sacrifice? Anything we have that takes our time away from him.

It's total commitment that God wants from us. The rest will fall into line as a matter of course.

Light Bulb Moment

Our connection with God is made stronger when we lift our hearts in praise to him.

Three-Part Harmony

GOD IS a master of exceptional beauty and order. In him we find rhythm, cadence, and splendor. He directs the earth to circle the sun, the moon to tug the seas, and the rivers to flow downhill.

Psalm 98:6 tells us:

> "With trumpets and sound of cornets make a joyful noise before the Lord, the King."

The noise that comes from our instruments is the music that lifts our hearts and souls into communion with the Father. We can find the very nature of our God in the songs we sing. His eternal aspect of three-in-one is revealed in the very music he desires us to lift unto him.

Musical Aspect No. 1:

All music is sound that is produced in an ordered structure. We call this the melody. We can ripple triplets across our keyboard, strum chords on our guitar, or toot a half note on our trombone; whatever method we choose, we imitate God, for he orders the world in a structure of his choosing.

Musical Aspect No. 2:

Great music is a choral activity. We combine various instruments, tones, and sounds. We sing according to our voices: soprano, alto, tenor, and bass. Just as we enjoy the interweaving harmony of the music, so God enjoys the harmony of his creation.

Musical Aspect No. 3:

The measured beat, the rhythm of the piece, carries the music along, creating pattern and drawing us in. The rhythm of the song is the heartbeat of the melody, allowing the music to come alive and envelop us with beauty and meaning. The rhythm of the sunrise and sunset, and the patterns of our daily lives are the cadence that accompanies us from birth until death, until we return to the Father who gave us life.

God is the Great Conductor of life. When we return our music of praise unto him, we acknowledge his sovereignty over all of creation and his presence in our very souls. It's in singing unto him that we truly become one with our Father above.

Our connection with God is made stronger when we lift our hearts in praise to him.

Light Bulb Moment

If we build God a palace without filling it with our praises, we have left the foundation stones undone.

What Do We Owe God?

PARENTING is a challenge. When we invite our children into the world, there are certain things we are obligated to provide for them. Food, clothing, and shelter are a few of them.

We don't question if we are obligated to feed our children. It's a right they have by the fact that they are ours. Even when they become adults, they can return for meals, emergency housing, and even clothing if they are in need.

Why? They are our children, and we always feel responsible for their care.

Now let's flip over the God coin. How does he see us as his children? We can find the start to our answer in 2 Samuel 7:1-29. It's quite a long passage, so let's pull out a portion of it.

Verse 2 has King David speaking to the prophet Nathan:

> "The king said to Nathan the prophet, 'See now, I dwell in a house of cedar, but the ark of God dwells in a tent.' "

His implication was that God should have a better house than a king, and to judge by our churches and synagogues, modern believers feel the same way. We build bigger and better in an attempt to glorify the great God of all creation.

Yet, who are we glorifying, God or ourselves? Let's look at God's reply in Verse 6:

> "I have not lived in a house since the day I brought up the people of Israel from Egypt to this day, but I have been moving about in a tent for my dwelling."

God goes on to say that he hasn't asked for a house to be built for him, neither will he fail to bless David and the children of Israel. His implication is that where he dwells is made holy by his presence. Having a grand cathedral fills us with pride, but God doesn't take notice of his surroundings. It's the worship of his people that gives him happiness.

God has an innate desire to give good things to his children. Just as we don't send our own children out to work for our benefit, so God doesn't require us to work to enable him to be glorious. Rather, he desires our worshipful heart and obedient spirit. When we worship him, even a tent can be the dwelling place of our King.

Solomon, David's son, did build a great temple unto God, but David knew the indwelling presence of the Lord in a tent. If all we have is a tent, God will fill us with his glory, and every step we take will reflect the majesty of his name.

If we build God a palace without filling it with our praises, we have left the foundation stones undone.

Light Bulb Moment

Our proof of our love for Christ is in the works we offer unto him.

Whom Do We Worship?

OF COURSE, we worship the Lord. Who else?

A contemporary entertainer was quoted as saying, "I was raised in the Church, but 85 percent of the people who attend are nonbelievers. They go because it's socially acceptable."

That's just one man's opinion, but the statement hits hard. Why? Because it has a ring of truth to it. It exposes the lack of faith found in today's churches. It's often easier to find faith in science, hard work, and a dependence on ourselves.

There's nothing wrong with science. It gives us our modern day comforts, explains much of the world around us, and enables the Church to broadcast the

Gospel around the world. As far as hard work? Even the Bible supports that.

It's dependence on ourselves that destroys the faith God wishes us to exemplify.

Jeremiah 22:14 asks:

> "Who says, 'I will build myself a great house with spacious upper rooms,' who cuts out windows for it, paneling it with cedar and painting it with vermilion?"

Much of the Lord's work on this earth is completed by the labor of our hands. The nonbeliever can raise up great institutions to do great good, just as the Church can. The difference is found in the giver's heart. The 85 percent who attend but don't believe, their offerings help support the work of the Lord, in spite of who places it in the offering plate.

Whom do we worship, God or man? Do we trust in the supreme intellect of an almighty Creator, or do we place our future in our human abilities?

Isaiah 41:19 states:

> "I will put in the wilderness the cedar, the aca-

cia, the myrtle, and the olive. I will set in the desert the cypress, the plane and the pine together, that they may see and know, may consider and understand together, that the hand of the Lord has done this, the Holy One of Israel has created it."

Even those of us who attend regularly need to reassess our lives and search our hearts and our motives. Why do we warm the pews each Sunday? Is it because others expect us to be there, or have we truly shown up to worship God? The pew will be warmed one way or another. Our offerings will fund God's work either way. The difference is in our hearts.

Matthew 2:11 reveals:

> "And going into the house they saw the child with Mary his mother, and they fell down and worshiped him. Then, opening their treasures, they offered him gifts, gold and frankincense and myrrh."

They fell down and worshipped him. With their hands, they offered their gifts. We can do the second without the first, but we can't do the first without the second. In the presence of the Lord, we have no other option.

Our proof of our love for Christ is in the works we offer unto him.

Coming to Christ
In Three Easy Steps

If you do not know Christ as your personal savior, there is no better time than the present to turn your life over to him.

- ➢ Step 1 is to admit that you are human, God is God, and you need his grace.
- ➢ Step 2 is to place your belief in him. You must accept that he is the Son of the Eternal God, and through his death on the cross, he can give you new life.
- ➢ Step 3 is to turn from your previous ways and receive the hope of Jesus' power in you.

Fill in the following information as a testament to your decision to accept Jesus as your Savior.

I, _____, accept Jesus
              print your full name

as my personal savior on _____.
                                   today's date

_____
                          your signature

Look for these additional topics on the MyChurchNotes.net website:

2 Timothy
Beatitudes
Discipleship
Evangelism
Faith
Family
Healing
Hope
Kingdom of God
Money
Prayer
Relationships
Repentance
Salvation
Worship

MyChurchNotes.net is a faith-based ministry founded on a belief in the Father, the Son, and the Holy Spirit. All MyChurchNotes.net articles are based on Scripture and created especially for MyChurchNotes.net.

Our Mission Statement is to take the Word of God into all the nations, and proclaim that he is Lord!

If you enjoyed
God Desires Worship From His People,
please visit us at our website:

www.MyChurchNotes.net

We look forward to hearing from you.

Website and Publication Powered by:

Bright Herd . . . for All Your Website and Media Design Needs.
www.brightherd.com
contact@brightherd.com

www.ingramcontent.com/pod-product-compliance
Lightning Source LLC
Chambersburg PA
CBHW070640050426
42451CB00008B/240